THE HARDEST HIDDEN PICTURES BOOK EVER

HIGHLIGHTS PRESS

Honesdale, Pennsylvania

THIS PRIZE IS FISHY

While Percy collects his prize, can you find all **22 hidden objects**?

banana

golf club

shuttlecock

binoculars

house

slice of pizza

book

magnet

spatula

boomerang

mallet

traffic light

boot

mushroom

wedge of lime

crown

needle

wizard's hat

envelope

paper airplane

frying pan

plunger

BONUS
Can you find 5 carnival tickets in this scene?

ART BY JEF CZE

TAKE TWO

Each of these scenes contains **12 hidden objects**, which are listed at the right. Find each object in one of the scenes, then cross it off the list.

Each object is hidden only once. Can you find them all?

adhesive bandage   drinking straw   iron   sailboat   spoon

banana   envelope   needle   saltshaker   teacup

candle   feather   paintbrush   slice of pie   toothbrush

carrot   heart   pencil   slice of pizza wedge of orange

comb   horseshoe   ruler   sock

SAY CHEESE!

There are **21 hidden objects** in and around this dinosaur. Can you find them all?

arrowhead

drinking straw

ladder

artist's brush

drumstick

mitten

boomerang

fish

mushroom

bowling ball

ghost

necktie

bowling pin

heart

paw print

cotton swab

ice-cream cone

pennant

crown

kite

sailboat

6

PHOTO BY MR1805/GETTYIMAGES • ART BY RICHARD POWE

6
BY SIX

Each of these small scenes contains **6 hidden objects** from the list below. Some objects are hidden in more than one scene. Can you find the 6 hidden objects in each scene?

HIDDEN OBJECT LIST

artist's brush (4)	lollipop (2)
bell (4)	mallet (2)
binoculars (3)	mitten (2)
crescent moon (4)	nail (3)
fishhook (3)	ruler (4)
ice-cream cone (3)	sock (2)

The numbers tell you how many times each object is hidden.

ART BY NEIL NUMBERMA

BONUS
Two scenes contain the exact same set of hidden objects. Can you find that matching pair?

JUST DUCKY

Not everyone minds the rain. Stay dry—or not!—as you search for these **16 hidden objects** in the scene.

artist's brush
book
candy corn
carrot
flag
fork

ice-cream cone
knitted hat
lollipop
needle
paintbrush
pear

pencil
ruler
shoe
spoon

ART BY MIKE DESAN

YODEL-AY-EE-OOOO!

The annual yodeling contest is in full swing. Plug your ears and grab your pencil! First use the secret code to figure out what objects are hidden in the scene. Then use that list to find the **19 hidden objects** in the big picture.

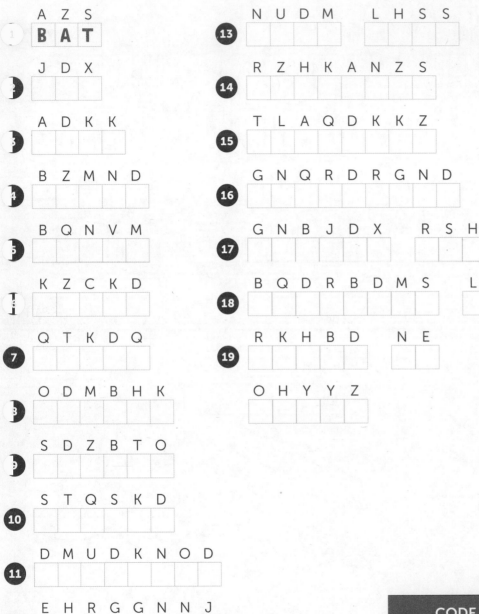

1. A Z S → **B A T**
2. J D X
3. A D K K
4. B Z M N D
5. B Q N V M
6. K Z C K D
7. Q T K D Q
8. O D M B H K
9. S D Z B T O
10. S T Q S K D
11. D M U D K N O D
12. E H R G G N N J
13. N U D M   L H S S
14. R Z H K A N Z S
15. T L A Q D K K Z
16. G N Q R D R G N D
17. G N B J D X   R S H B J
18. B Q D R B D M S   L N N M
19. R K H B D   N E

O H Y Y Z

CODE CRACKER

Each letter in the code is the letter in the alphabet that comes before the real letter. So, for example, an A in the code would be a *B* for real. And the code word CNF would stand for *DOG*. Also, in this code, a *Z* stands for an *A*.

ART BY MIKE DESANTIS

SUPER CHALLENGE!

There are **30 hidden objects** in this mall. Without clues or knowing what to look for, try to find them all.

IT'S SPRINKLING

There are **18 crayons** hiding among these sprinkles. Can you find them all?

PHOTOS BY VASKO/ISTOCK (SPRINKLES) AND DLERICK/ISTOCK (CRAYONS) • ART BY BILL GOLLIHER

TURTLE POND

Find the **28 objects** in this scene.

acorn
banana
bell
bowl
butter knife
can
candle
carrot
flashlight
flower

golf club
heart
high-heeled shoe
horseshoe
lightning bolt
lollipop
nail
pencil
pennant
ring

ruler
saucepan
slice of bread
slice of pizza
sock
tack
three-leaf clover
traffic cone

ART BY DIANA ZOURELIAS

OTTER OLYMPICS

These otters are trying to win the gold medal in synchronized swimming. You can go for the gold by searching for all **20 hidden objects** in the scene.

adhesive bandage

kite

ruler

arrowhead

megaphone

slice of bread

candle

paper clip

slice of pizza

domino

party hat

tea bag

drumstick

paw print

tennis ball

envelope

pencil

worm

heart

question mark

BONUS
Can you find 5 ladybugs in this scene?

ART BY PATRICK GIROUA

TAKE TWO

Each of these scenes contains **12 hidden objects**, which are listed at the right. Find each object in one of the scenes, then cross it off the list.

ART BY JEF CZEKAJ

Each object is hidden only once. Can you find them all?

banana	dolphin	frying pan	leaf	scissors
bird	envelope	funnel	mug	screwdriver
canoe	feather	hockey stick	pencil	shuttlecock
chef's hat	fishhook	ice-cream cone	plunger	wedge of cheese
desk bell	flashlight	ice skate	saltshaker	

BRANCH OUT

Go out on a limb to find **24 hidden objects** in and under this tree.

artist's brush

ghost

pennant

bat

golf tee

pointy hat

bell

hanger

shuttlecock

bowling ball

heart

slice of pizza

candy corn

ice-cream cone

snake

cane

mushroom

swim fin

crown

necktie

tooth

fish

needle

umbrella

22

BY SIX

Each of these small scenes contains **6 hidden objects** from the list below. Some objects are hidden in more than one scene. Can you find the 6 hidden objects in each scene?

HIDDEN OBJECT LIST

bolt (4)	needle (2)
crescent moon (3)	paper airplane (2)
drinking straw (3)	pencil (4)
jelly bean (2)	piece of popcorn (4)
mitten (2)	slice of pie (4)
mushroom (3)	spoon (3)

The numbers tell you how many times each object is hidden.

ART BY NEIL NUMBERMA

BONUS
Two scenes contain the exact same set of hidden objects. Can you find that matching pair?

rEADY, SET, BOWL!

It's time to roll some strikes and find the **16 hidden objects** in this scene.

butterfly
carrot
cherries
crown
drinking straw
golf club

hatchet
magic wand
oven mitt
pear
pillow
ring

slice of pizza
spatula
toothbrush
tube of toothpaste

LIZARD LAUGHS

Time for school—and to learn a joke! Use the clues below to figure out the words. Each word is a hidden object to look for in the big scene. Once you've found all **14 hidden objects** transfer the letters with numbers into the correct spaces to discover the punch line to the joke.

1 *The Cat in the*

___ ___ ___
   1

2 Put cereal in this.

___ ___ ___ ___
    2

3 A nickel, dime, or penny

___ ___ ___ ___
    3

4 Put this on after your sock.

___ ___ ___ ___
    4

5 A mitten with fingers

___ ___ ___ ___
   5

6 It pumps blood through your body.

___ ___ ___ ___ ___
  6

7 A yellow fruit that's often sliced on cereal

___ ___ ___ ___ ___ ___
    7

8 A shirt fastener

___ ___ ___ ___ ___
  8

9 Use this in a coloring book.

___ ___ ___ ___ ___ ___
   9

10 The *P* in PB&J

___ ___ ___ ___ ___ ___
     10

11 A sport with touchdowns

___ ___ ___ ___ ___ ___ ___ ___
    11

12 A red-and-white-striped Christmas treat.

___ ___ ___ ___ ___   ___ ___ ___ ___
      12

13 Cook eggs and bacon in this.

___ ___ ___ ___ ___ ___ ___
       13

14 Use this to score a goal on ice.

___ ___ ___ ___ ___   ___ ___ ___ ___ ___
      14

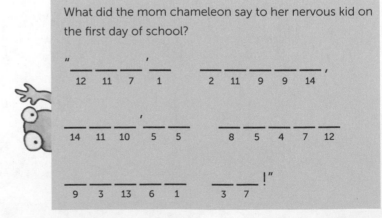

What did the mom chameleon say to her nervous kid on the first day of school?

" ___ ___ ___ ___ ' ___ ___ ___ ___ ,
  12 11 7 1   2 11 9 9 14

___ ___ ___ ___ ' ___   ___ ___ ___ ___
14 11 10 5 5   8 5 4 7 12

___ ___ ___ ___ ___   ___ ___ !"
9 3 13 6 1   3 7

28

SUPER CHALLENGE!

There are **30 hidden objects** in this camping scene. Without clues or knowing what to look for, try to find them all.

30

LOST ACRES CAMPGROUND

I LOVE BERRIES!

PHOTO BY FLORIANTM/GETTYIMAGES • ART BY BILL GOLLI

OUT-OF-THIS-WORLD PIZZA

This pizza is worth waiting for! While the astronauts get ready to dig in, see if you can find all **23 hidden objects** in this scene.

artist's brush

horn

scissors

boomerang

horseshoe

snake

boot

ice-cream cone

spoon

closed umbrella

key

stick of gum

envelope

mallet

three-leaf clover

fish

paper clip

toothbrush

fork

ring

whistle

fried egg

ruler

BONUS
Can you find 5 arrows in this scene?

34

TAKE TWO

Each of these scenes contains **12 hidden objects**, which are listed at the right. Find each object in one of the scenes, then cross it off the list.

ART BY DAVE KLUG

Each object is hidden only once. Can you find them all?

banana	crown	kite	pennant	slice of pizza
bell	fish	ladle	plum	sock
candle	fishhook	mushroom	rake	toothbrush
carrot	eyeglasses	paintbrush	ring	wishbone
crayon	golf club	paper clip	sailboat	

BEST FRIENDS FUR-EVER

Sit, stay, and see if you can fetch the **14 hidden objects** in this scene.

baseball
cap

fish

needle

book

fishhook

piece of
popcorn

bowl

heart

shoe

crescent
moon

kite

spoon

crown

necktie

6 BY SIX

Each of these small scenes contains **6 hidden objects** from the list below. Some objects are hidden in more than one scene. Can you find the 6 hidden objects in each scene?

HIDDEN OBJECT LIST

comb (3)	pitcher (3)
drumstick (4)	slice of pizza (2)
flashlight (3)	teacup (3)
lollipop (2)	toothbrush (3)
mitten (3)	waffle (2)
nail (3)	yo-yo (5)

The numbers tell you how many times each object is hidden.

BONUS
Two scenes contain the exact same set of hidden objects. Can you find that matching pair?

ALMOST THERE

These cross-country teams know the meaning of "slow and steady." You should pace yourself as you find each of the **16 hidden objects** in this scene.

- artist's brush
- bowl
- carrot
- comb
- crown
- fish
- mitten
- paper clip
- pencil
- ruler
- sailboat
- slice of bacon
- slice of pizza
- tennis racket
- toothbrush
- vase

ART BY DAVE KL

HAPPY MOM'S DAY!

Mom is going to love breakfast in bed! While she eats, you can clean up this puzzle. First use the secret code to figure out what objects are hidden in the scene. Then use that list to find the **16 hidden objects** in the big picture.

1. W Q K → **K E Y**

2. R U E T → F I S H

3. D U Z S → R I N G

4. S X A H Q → G L O V E

5. O D M K A Z → C R A Y O N

6. B Q M Z G F → P E A N U T

7. S A X R O X G N → G O L F C L U B

8. E G U F O M E Q → S U I T C A S E

9. N A I X U Z S B U Z → B O W L I N G P I N

10. O A M F T M Z S Q D → C O A T H A N G E R

11. Q K Q S X M E E Q E → E Y E G L A S S E S

12. R X M E T X U S T F → F L A S H L I G H T

13. E W U S A S S X Q E → S K I G O G G L E S

14. I D U E F I M F O T → W R I S T W A T C H

15. N M E Q N M X X N M F → B A S E B A L L B A T

16. B M U D A R B M Z F E → P A I R O F P A N T S

CODE CRACKER

A=O	J=X	S=G
B=P	K=Y	T=H
C=Q	L=Z	U=I
D=R	M=A	V=J
E=S	N=B	W=K
F=T	O=C	X=L
G=U	P=D	Y=M
H=V	Q=E	Z=N
I=W	R=F	

Happy
Mother's
Day

SUPER CHALLENGE!

There are **30 hidden objects** in this scene. Without clues or knowing what to look for, try to find them all.

ART BY PAULA BECKER

THAT'S OIL, FOLKS

Can you spot the **20 number 3's** hidden in this photo of oil and water?

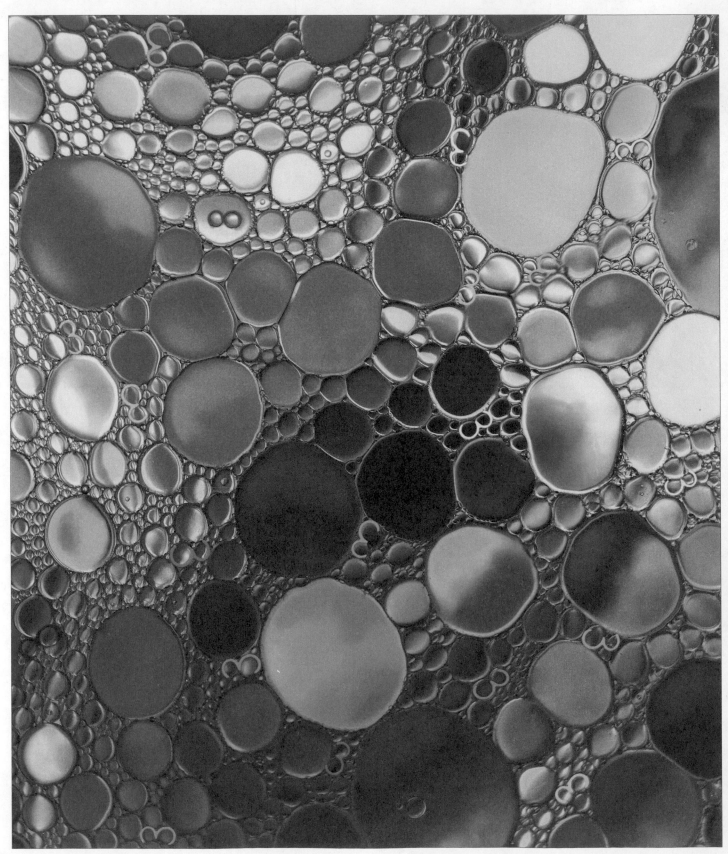

PHOTO BY EUREKA_89/GETTYIMAGES • ART BY BILL GOLLIHER

GOING TO THE DOGS

Find the **32 objects** in this scene.

banana
bean
bowl
bowling ball
butter knife
can
carrot
caterpillar
cotton candy
crescent moon
crown

fishhook
four-leaf clover
frying pan
funnel
glove
golf tee
heart
ice-cream cone
lollipop
magnet
mushroom

nail
needle
oilcan
peanut
pencil
piece of popcorn
ring
sailboat
slice of pie
wedge of lemon

ART BY DIANA ZOURELIAS

SWIM ON IN

Make a splash and see if you can find the **22 hidden objects** in this scene.

 banana

 golf club

 pennant

 bottle

 heart

 ring

 bowl

 ice-cream cone

 ruler

 bowling ball

 mitten

 sailboat

 butter knife

 mug

 shoe

 cinnamon bun

 mushroom

 slice of pizza

 domino

 olive

 envelope

 paper clip

BONUS
Can you find 5 pairs of swimming goggles in this scene?

ART BY RICH POWE

TAKE TWO

Each of these scenes contains **12 hidden objects**, which are listed at the right. Find each object in one of the scenes, then cross it off the list.

Each object is hidden only once. Can you find them all?

anchor

banana

bat

book

cane

canoe

cupcake

drinking straw

glove

hammer

harmonica

ice-cream cone

ladder

magnet

mushroom

paintbrush

pencil

ruler

skateboard

slice of cake

sock

toaster

toothbrush

yo-yo

GOING IN CIRCLES

Look around this carousel. Can you find the **18 hidden objects** riding on it?

hot dog

artist's brush

needle

domino

ice-cream cone

shoe

dustpan

kite

slice of pie

fish

light bulb

slice of pizza

fried egg

mug

train

hammer

mushroom

tulip

54

6

BY SIX

Each of these small scenes contains **6 hidden objects** from the list below. Some objects are hidden in more than one scene. Can you find the 6 hidden objects in each scene?

HIDDEN OBJECT LIST

artist's brush (4)	fish (2)
banana (3)	pencil (3)
button (3)	ring (3)
crescent moon (3)	sock (2)
drinking straw (3)	toothbrush (3)
envelope (4)	yo-yo (2)

The numbers tell you how many times each object is hidden.

BONUS
Two scenes contain the exact same set of hidden objects. Can you find that matching pair?

SPACE SCHOOL

The Intergalactic Space School has students from all over the galaxy—and beyond! While they board the bus, you can study the scene for **16 hidden objects**.

apple
banana
baseball bat
bell
broccoli
crayon

fish
golf club
hockey stick
lollipop
mitten
needle

ruler
saucepan
slice of bread
toothbrush

THE BIG GAME

It's the first annual Sloth Table Tennis Tournament and you have a front-row seat! First use the secret code to figure out what objects are hidden in the scene. Then use that list to find the **17 hidden objects** in the big picture.

1. N V H → M U G

2. C P P U

3. C P X M

4. D P N C

5. D S B C

6. G J T I

7. I F B S U

8. S V M F S

9. D B O E M F

10. G V O O F M

11. N J U U F O

12. F M G'T   I B U

13. T F B   T U B S

14. G P P U C B M M

15. T D J T T P S T

16. Q B Q F S   D M J Q

17. C P X M J O H   C B M M

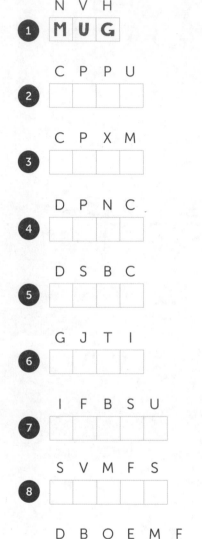

SUPER CHALLENGE!

There are **30 hidden objects** in this scene. Without clues or knowing what to look for, try to find them all.

ART BY PAULA BECKER

PROUD AS A PEACOCK

There are **21 lime wedges** in this beautiful bird. Can you find them all?

FUNNY FOOTBALL

Randall came so close to making the catch! You can save the game if you can find all **18 hidden objects** listed below.

banana

horn

sailboat

book

horseshoe

saw

comb

light bulb

shovel

fishhook

mitten

sock

golf club

paper clip

teacup

hockey stick

pencil

toothbrush

BONUS
Can you find 5 water bottles in this scene?

TAKE TWO

Each of these scenes contains **12 hidden objects**, which are listed at the right. Find each object in one of the scenes, then cross it off the list.

Each object is hidden only once. Can you find them all?

apple   carrot   giraffe   pear   snake

~~artist's brush~~ crown   hedgehog   pyramid   toothbrush

ax   eggplant   key   rubber duck   wedge of cheese

baseball bat   envelope   light bulb   ruler   wristwatch

bell   fork   lizard   saltshaker

TEST THE WATERS

Put on your goggles and find the
17 hidden objects in this scene.

apple

dog bone

mushroom

bell

glove

pencil

boomerang

hatchet

sailboat

canoe

high-heeled
shoe

slice of
pizza

carrot

hourglass

wishbone

cupcake

light bulb

PHOTO BY VLAD61/GETTYIMAGES • ART BY KEN KRU

6
BY SIX

Each of these small scenes contains **6 hidden objects** from the list below. Some objects are hidden in more than one scene. Can you find the 6 hidden objects in each scene?

HIDDEN OBJECT LIST

candle (4)	slice of cake (3)
fish (2)	slice of pizza (4)
glove (3)	snail (2)
needle (3)	surfboard (4)
ladder (2)	toothbrush (3)
pencil (4)	waffle (2)

The numbers tell you how many times each object is hidden.

ART BY KELLY KENNED

BONUS
Two scenes contain the exact same set of hidden objects. Can you find that matching pair?

WHEEL FUN

The skate park is the place to be today—especially if you want to find hidden objects! Look for each of the **17 hidden objects** in this scene.

artist's brush	heart	slice of pizza
baby's bottle	hoe	spoon
banana	ice-cream cone	toothbrush
candy cane	kite	umbrella
envelope	paintbrush	wedge of lemon
flashlight		
hat		

FLYING IN THE RAIN

How do birds fly in the rain? To find out, first use the clues below to figure out the words. Each word is a hidden object to look for in the big scene. Once you've found the **14 hidden objects** transfer the letters with numbers into the correct spaces to learn the punch line to the joke.

1 You wear one on your finger.

___ ___ ___ ___
　　　　1

2 You might wish upon one at night.

___ ___ ___ ___
　　　　2

3 Where a baseball batter stands: home _____

___ ___ ___ ___ ___
　　3

4 Postage to mail a letter

___ ___ ___ ___ ___
　　　　　4

5 Neckwear for a tuxedo

___ ___ ___ ___　　___ ___ ___
　　　5

6 A small, red fruit with a pit

___ ___ ___ ___ ___
　　　6

7 Snickerdoodle or chocolate chip

___ ___ ___ ___ ___ ___
　　　　7

8 Thread this to sew.

___ ___ ___ ___ ___
　　　　8

9 The *T* in a BLT sandwich

___ ___ ___ ___ ___ ___
　　9

10 A hot-air _____

___ ___ ___ ___ ___ ___ ___ ___
　　　　　　　　10

11 A small, frosted treat, often given at birthday parties

___ ___ ___ ___ ___ ___
　　　11

12 Throw this toy and it will come back to you.

___ ___ ___ ___ ___ ___ ___ ___
　　　　　　12

13 Hang one above the stable door for good luck.

___ ___ ___ ___ ___ ___ ___
　　　　　　13

14 A goalie slaps away shots with this.

___ ___ ___ ___ ___　　___ ___ ___ ___
　　　　　14

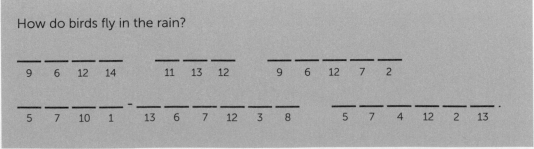

How do birds fly in the rain?

___ ___ ___ ___　　___ ___ ___　　___ ___ ___ ___ ___
9　6　12　14　　11　13　12　　9　6　12　7　2

___ ___ ___ ___ - ___ ___ ___ ___ ___ ___　　___ ___ ___ ___ ___ ___.
5　7　10　1　　13　6　7　12　3　8　　　5　7　4　12　2　13

SUPER CHALLENGE!

There are **30 hidden objects** in this library. Without clues or knowing what to look for, try to find them all.

ART BY DARYLL COLLINS

GONE FISHIN'

This coral fan is hiding **20 fish.** Can you find each one?

PIGSTY PLAY

Find the **33 objects** in this scene.

banana
basket
bean
bell
bowl
butterfly
button
carrot
coin
cracker
crescent moon

elf's hat
envelope
fish
flag
fried egg
golf tee
heart
jar
lollipop
magnet
mitten

piece of popcorn
ring
sailboat
shoe
shuttlecock
slice of pizza
snake
tack
teacup
wedge of lemon
wrench

ART BY DIANA ZOURELIAS

EXTRA CHEESE, PLEASE!

Muttzarella's has the best pizza in town. Can you fetch all **22 hidden objects**?

 arrow

 game piece

 ring

 banana

 golf club

 sailboat

 carrot

 heart

 slice of pie

 caterpillar

 lollipop

 snail

 comb

 mitten

 spoon

 eyeglasses

 mushroom

 toothbrush

 feather

 penguin

BONUS
Can you find 5 dog bones in this scene?

 flashlight

 pitchfork

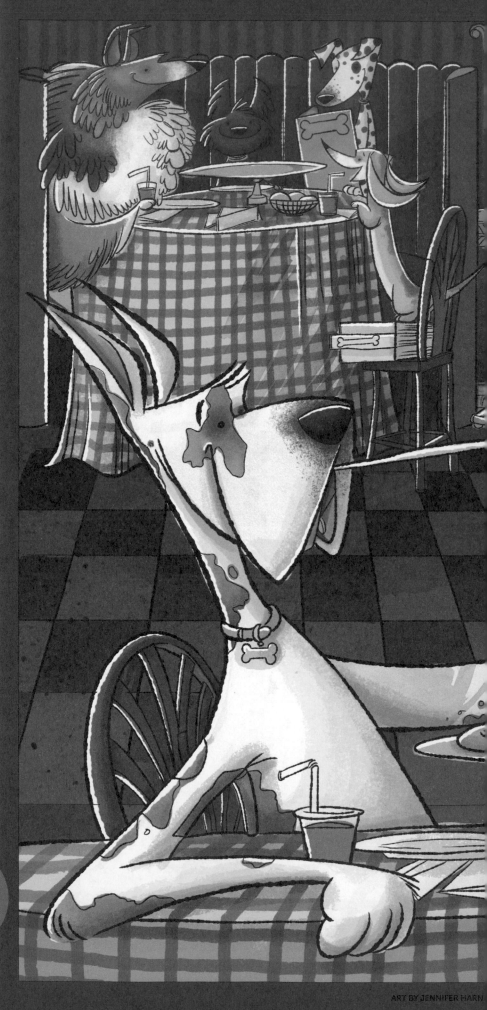

TAKE TWO

Each of these scenes contains **12 hidden objects**, which are listed at the right. Find each object in one of the scenes, then cross it off the list.

ART BY KELLY KENNEDY

Each object is hidden only once. Can you find them all?

artist's brush

banana

boomerang

boot

canoe

chili pepper

doughnut

envelope

fish

flashlight

fork

glove

heart

ladder

pencil

sailboat

slice of pizza

star

tent

toothbrush

waffle

wagon

wedge of lemon

yo-yo

85

FLOATING ON AIR

Can you find the **16 hidden objects** on and around these hot-air balloons?

artist's brush

fish

pumpkin

banana

football

saw

bowling pin

heart

shovel

candle

lemon

slipper

dog bone

megaphone

umbrella

open book

PHOTO BY ANEESE/GETTYIMAGES • ART BY KEN KRUG

6 BY SIX

Each of these small scenes contains **6 hidden objects** from the list below. Some objects are hidden in more than one scene. Can you find the 6 hidden objects in each scene?

HIDDEN OBJECT LIST

banana (3)	hockey stick (2)
bolt (4)	horseshoe (4)
candle (3)	muffin (2)
envelope (4)	pencil (4)
fish (4)	slice of bread (2)
flowerpot (2)	slice of cake (2)

The numbers tell you how many times each object is hidden.

88

BONUS
Two scenes contain the exact same set of hidden objects. Can you find that matching pair?

SNOWBOARD SAFARI

These animals are on vacation. Can you find **16 hidden objects** in this scene?

artist's brush
boomerang
canoe
carrot
comb

crescent moon
fish
fishhook
football
heart

key
mushroom
ring
ruler
slice of pizza
teacup

SLOW DOWN!

What is the dog saying to the cat? To find out, first use the clues below to figure out the words. Each word is a hidden object to look for in the big scene. Once you've found the **12 hidden objects**, transfer the letters with numbers into the correct spaces to learn the punch line to the joke.

1. Use this to chop wood.

__ __
1

2. A tool to wash floors

__ __ __
2

3. The Liberty _____

__ __ __ __
3

4. A cod or a guppy

__ __ __ __
4

5. A popular flavor of pie

__ __ __ __ __
5

6. The biggest mammal in the ocean

__ __ __ __ __
6

7. A baked treat similar to a cupcake

__ __ __ __ __ __
7

8. It can be baked or mashed.

__ __ __ __ __
8

9. "Frosty the _____"

__ __ __ __ __ __ __
9

10. Rock, paper, _____

__ __ __ __ __ __ __
10

11. Use it to spread color on a wall.

__ __ __ __ __ __ __ __ __
11

12. Fold this toy by hand and then fly it.

__ __ __ __ __ __ __ __ __
12

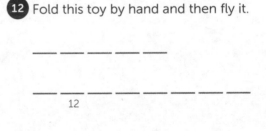

What did the police dog say to the speeder?

"__ __ __ __   __ __   __ __ __
  10 8 2 5   12 7   8 11 3

__ __ __ __   __ __   __ __ __
 7 1 9 3   2 4   8 11 3

__ __ __!"
 5 1 6

ART BY MIKE MOR

OPEN

MAIN ST.

SUPER CHALLENGE!

There are **30 hidden objects** in this science museum. Without clues or knowing what to look for, try to find them all.

ART BY PAULA BECKER

GO WITH THE FLOW

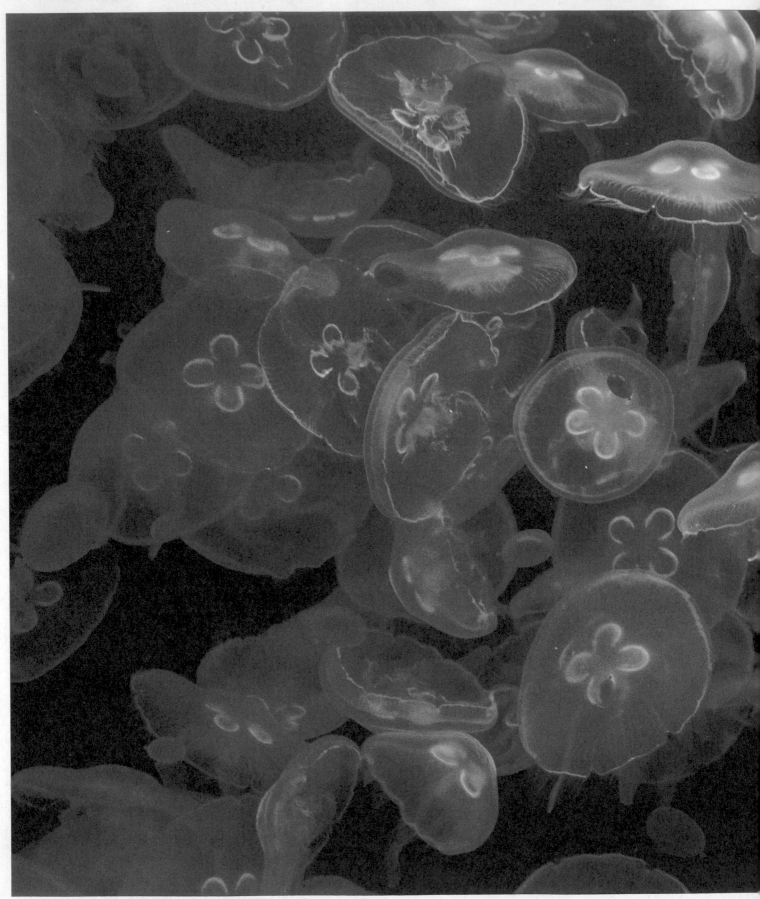

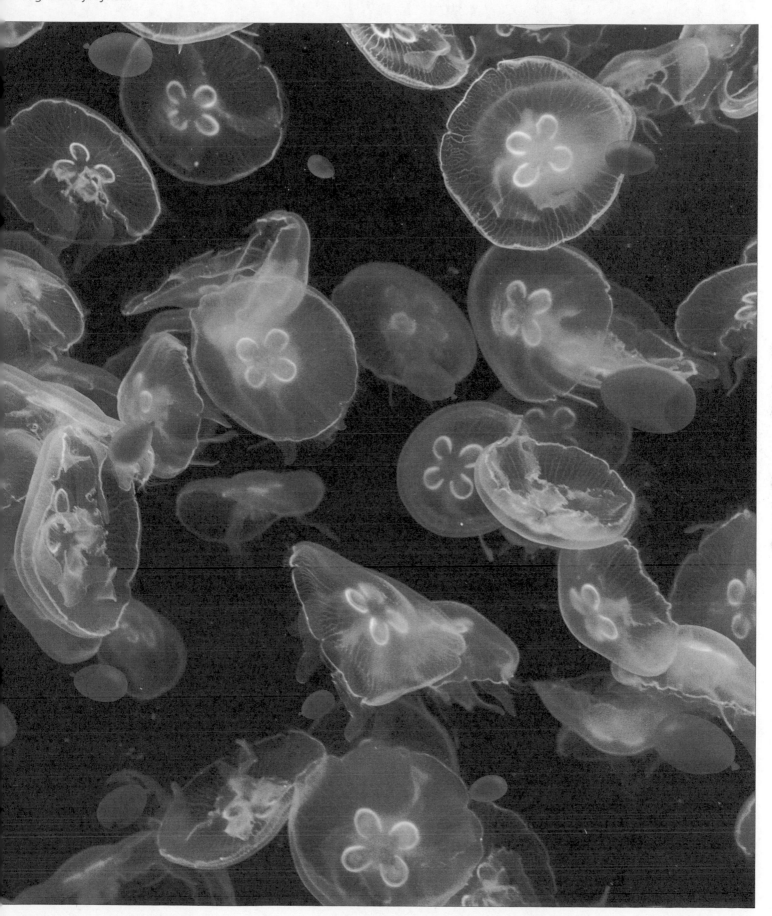

Can you pick out the
2 balloons hiding
among these jellyfish?

PRESTO
PANDA

Hocus-pocus! Can you make all **20 hidden objects** appear before your very eyes?

artist's brush

fork

needle

candle

golf club

recorder

candy cane

heart

safety pin

carrot

ice-cream scoop

telescope

drinking straw

lollipop

tweezers

fishing pole

mitten

wedge of lime

football

mushroom

BONUS
Can you find 5 magician's wands in this scene?

ART BY JEF CZEKA

TAKE TWO

Each of these scenes contains **12 hidden objects**, which are listed at the right. Find each object in one of the scenes, then cross it off the list.

Each object is hidden only once. Can you find them all?

acorn

artist's brush

banana

boomerang

butterfly

button

candle

clothespin

crayon

crescent moon

crown

domino

fish

frog

hammer

heart

hedgehog

ladle

mitten

orange

pencil

puzzle piece

ruler

sailboat

SNOW FUN

Jump in and search for the **16 hidden objects** in this scene.

artist's brush

ice-cream cone

toothbrush

banana

kite

turtle

baseball bat

mushroom

umbrella

flowerpot

shark

window

fork

slice of cake

wrench

slice of pizza

PHOTO BY MEL·NIK/GETTYIMAGES • ART BY KEN KRU

6
BY SIX

Each of these small scenes contains **6 hidden objects** from the list below. Some objects are hidden in more than one scene. Can you find the 6 hidden objects in each scene?

HIDDEN OBJECT LIST

acorn (4)	hairbrush (2)
button (3)	mallet (3)
canoe (3)	needle (3)
comb (3)	sailboat (4)
domino (3)	saucepan (2)
drinking straw (4)	wishbone (2)

The numbers tell you how many times each object is hidden.

BONUS
Two scenes contain the exact same set of hidden objects. Can you find that matching pair?

A WHALE OF A TIME

While Willie watches whales, will you watch for hidden objects? See if you can spot all **16 hidden objects** in this scene.

banana
baseball cap
can
candle
crescent moon
eyeglasses

golf club
heart
ice-cream cone
mug
nail
needle

pencil
pumpkin
ruler
toothbrush

ART BY MIKE DESANT

HOP TO IT!

Jump in and solve this puzzle! First use the secret code to figure out what objects are hidden in the scene. Then use the list to find the **14 hidden objects** in the big picture.

1. Y Z G
   B A T

2. X Z I

3. X L N Y

4. U L I P

5. X I L D M

6. S V Z I G

7. I F O V I

8. X Z M W O V

9. U F M M V O

10. M V V W O V

11. G V Z X F K

12. G S R N Y O V

13. S L X P V B
    H G R X P

14. X I V H X V M G
    N L L M

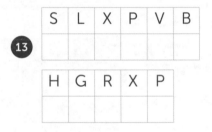

CODE CRACKER

A=Z	H=S	O=L	V=E
B=Y	I=R	P=K	W=D
C=X	J=Q	Q=J	X=C
D=W	K=P	R=I	Y=B
E=V	L=O	S=H	Z=A
F=U	M=N	T=G	
G=T	N=M	U=F	

ART BY RICK STROMOSKI

SUPER CHALLENGE!

There are **30 hidden objects** in this pool scene. Without clues or knowing what to look for, try to find them all.

ART BY DARYLL COLLINS

PICNIC POST

This picnic has more than just food. There are also **20 envelopes**. Can you find them all?

PHOTO BY DEMAREE/ISTOCK • ART BY BILL GOLLIHER

PLANETARIUM DAY

Find the **29 objects** in this scene.

- banana
- bean
- bell
- book
- bowl
- butterfly
- crayon
- doughnut
- flag
- flowerpot
- funnel
- golf tee
- heart
- hockey stick
- ice-cream cone
- lollipop
- magnet
- pencil
- potato
- rolling pin
- sailboat
- saucepan
- shuttlecock
- slice of pizza
- spool of thread
- stick of gum
- teacup
- wishbone
- yo-yo

ART BY DIANA ZOURELIAS

MERRY MOWING

Grace's favorite chore is mowing the lawn. While she mows, can you track down all **22 hidden objects**?

anchor

fish

open book

ball of yarn

glove

paper airplane

banana

high-heeled shoe

pencil

button

ice-cream bar

puzzle piece

chili pepper

mitten

slice of pizza

coat hanger

mug

wedge of orange

comb

necklace

crescent moon

needle

BONUS
Can you find 5 butterflies in this scene?

ART BY IRYNA BODNAR

TAKE TWO

Each of these scenes contains **12 hidden objects**, which are listed at the right. Find each object in one of the scenes, then cross it off the list.

ART BY BRIAN WHITE

Each object is hidden only once. Can you find them all?

banana

candle

cane

~~carrot~~

crown

envelope

fishhook

fried egg

glove

golf club

heart

horseshoe

ice-cream cone

paper clip

paper airplane

pear

pencil

ring

ruler

slice of pie

strawberry

tent

toothbrush

wedge of lime

MONKEYING AROUND

Go bananas and find the **17 hidden objects** in this photo.

banana   fish   needle

bird   fishhook   pennant

boomerang   heart   sailboat

canoe   high-heeled shoe   shovel

comb   ice-cream cone   slice of pizza

crescent moon   mug

PHOTO BY KCHANDE/GETTYIMAGES • ART BY RICH POWELL

6
BY SIX

Each of these small scenes contains **6 hidden objects** from the list below. Some objects are hidden in more than one scene. Can you find the 6 hidden objects in each scene?

HIDDEN OBJECT LIST

ax (4)	heart (3)
candle (3)	needle (3)
carrot (2)	mitten (3)
crayon (3)	paper airplane (2)
crescent moon (4)	pepper (3)
crown (4)	toothbrush (2)

The numbers tell you how many times each object is hidden.

BONUS
Two scenes contain the exact same set of hidden objects. Can you find that matching pair?

121

SHE SHOOTS, SHE SCORES!

The Penguin Pucksters are about to win the game! Can you find **16 hidden objects** in this scene?

boot
candle
crescent moon
drinking straw
flashlight
hammer

ladder
magnifying glass
pen
pencil
pennant
pineapple

sailboat
saltshaker
sock
toothbrush

ACRO-CATS

While these cat gymnasts practice purr-fect form, you can solve this puzzle. First use the clues below to figure out the words. Each word is a hidden object to look for in the big scene. Once you've found the **13 hidden objects**, transfer the letters with numbers into the correct spaces to learn the punch line to the joke.

1 A salmon or a trout

___ ___ ___ ___
     1

2 There are 50 stars on the U.S. _____.

___ ___ ___ ___
     2

3 Twirl spaghetti with this.

___ ___ ___ ___
   3

4 "And a partridge in a _____ tree."

___ ___ ___ ___
3

5 A king's headwear

___ ___ ___ ___
5

6 A monkey's favorite fruit

___ ___ ___ ___ ___
       6

7 Put it on a one-year-old's birthday cake.

___ ___ ___ ___ ___
       7

8 A long orange vegetable

___ ___ ___ ___ ___ ___
       8

9 Pound nails with this.

___ ___ ___ ___ ___
     9

10 Write with this at school.

___ ___ ___ ___ ___ ___
      10

11 A "sunny-side-up" breakfast food

___ ___ ___ ___ ___   ___ ___ ___
        11

12 Put this up when it rains.

___ ___ ___ ___ ___ ___ ___ ___
12

13 Use this to hit a puck.

___ ___ ___ ___ ___ ___   ___ ___ ___ ___
                         13

How do you get a cat to do tricks?

___ ___ ___   ___   ___ ___ ___   ___ ___
 4 12 8   6   11 3 2   13 10

___   ___ ___ ___   ___ ___ ___ ___ ___ ___.
 6   5 6 8   5 3 1 8 12 9 7

125

SUPER CHALLENGE!

There are **30 hidden objects** in this auditorium. Without clues or knowing what to look for, try to find them all.

ART BY PAULA BECKER

SOMETHING'S FISHY

These leaves are
hiding **15 goldfish**.
Can you find them all?

MAGIC HAT DINER

Abracadabra! Just like magic, **20 hidden objects** have been hidden inside this diner. Can you find each one?

book

envelope

paper clip

boomerang

fish

pencil

butterfly

fishhook

plunger

carrot

flashlight

sailboat

closed umbrella

golf club

sock

comb

horn

tube of paint

crown

mitten

BONUS
Can you find 5 aces of spades in this scene?

130

TAKE TWO

Each of these scenes contains **12 hidden objects**, which are listed at the right. Find each object in one of the scenes, then cross it off the list.

Each object is hidden only once. Can you find them all?

anchor

banana

crown

dog bone

~~drinking straw~~

drumstick

dustpan

envelope

feather

fork

grapes

hockey stick

ladder

ladle

light bulb

nail

needle

paper airplane

paper clip

party hat

ring

sock

toothbrush

wedge of cheese

HELLO, ELLIE

This wise elephant is hiding **10 hidden objects**. Can you find them all?

bird

shoe

comb

snail

feather

sock

lizard

whale

mushroom

wishbone

PHOTO BY MILOSJOKIC/ISTOCK • ART BY RICHARD POWEL

AGES 2–3

PAGES 10–11

DRY GOODS & SUNDRIES

PAGES 4–5

PAGES 12–13

1. bat	13. oven mitt
2. key	14. sailboat
3. bell	15. umbrella
4. canoe	16. horseshoe
5. crown	17. hockey stick
6. ladle	18. crescent moon
7. ruler	19. slice of pizza
8. pencil	
9. teacup	
10. turtle	
11. envelope	
12. fishhook	

PAGES 6–7

PAGES 14–15

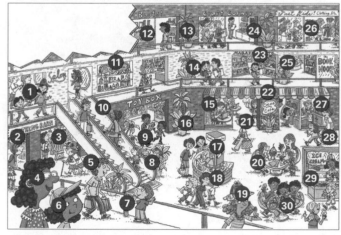

1. paper clip	11. belt	21. ladle
2. pencil	12. crescent moon	22. ladder
3. vase	13. hoe	23. fork
4. candy cane	14. crown	24. ruler
5. kite	15. baby's rattle	25. scissors
6. lollipop	16. football	26. spool of thread
7. baseball bat	17. whistle	27. banana
8. star	18. carrot	28. lock
9. crayon	19. cupcake	29. candle
10. cane	20. fish	30. wedge of lemon

PAGES 8–9

PAGE 16

PAGE 17

PAGES 18-19

PAGES 20-21

PAGES 22-23

PAGES 24-25

PAGES 26-27

PAGES 28-29

1. hat
2. bowl
3. coin
4. shoe
5. glove
6. heart
7. banana
8. button
9. crayon
10. peanut
11. football
12. candy cane
13. frying pan
14. hockey stick

What did the mom chameleon say to her nervous kid on the first day of school?

"Don't worry, you'll blend right in!"

1. saw
2. spoon
3. teacup
4. banana peel
5. handbag
6. hat
7. thimble
8. sock
9. comb
10. cupcake

11. crescent moon
12. shoe
13. boomerang
14. can
15. ruler
16. envelope
17. fish
18. arrow
19. candy cane
20. magnifying glass

21. golf club
22. lollipop
23. ring
24. pencil
25. seashell
26. crown
27. slice of pizza
28. yo-yo
29. ice-cream cone
30. button

PAGES 32–33

PAGES 34–35

PAGES 36–37

PAGES 38–39

PAGES 40–41

PAGES 42–43

PAGES 44–45

1. key
2. fish
3. ring
4. glove
5. crayon
6. peanut
7. golf club
8. suitcase
9. bowling pin
10. coat hanger
11. eyeglasses
12. flashlight
13. ski goggles
14. wristwatch
15. baseball bat
16. pair of pants

PAGES 46–47

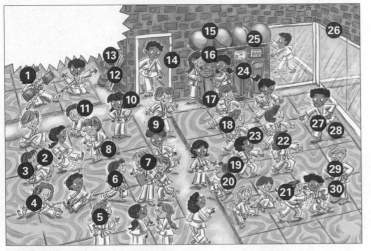

1. fork
2. heart
3. crown
4. muffin
5. fried egg
6. artist's brush
7. crescent moon
8. pencil
9. teacup
10. sock
11. ladle
12. needle
13. ring
14. drinking straw
15. funnel
16. envelope
17. banana
18. fish
19. saltshaker
20. glove
21. leaf
22. apple
23. worm
24. cane
25. slice of pie
26. ruler
27. spoon
28. flashlight
29. slice of pizza
30. wishbone

PAGE 48

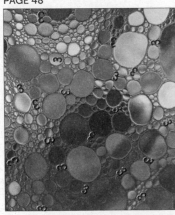

PAGE 49

PAGES 50–51

PAGES 52–53

PAGES 54–55

PAGES 56–57

ANSWERS

1. mug
2. boot
3. bowl
4. comb
5. crab
6. fish
7. heart
8. ruler
9. candle
10. funnel
11. mitten
12. elf's hat
13. sea star
14. football
15. scissors
16. paper clip
17. bowling ball

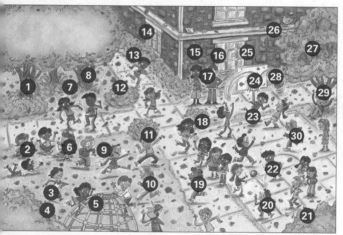

1. baseball bat
2. saltshaker
3. pencil
4. teacup
5. candle
6. pear
7. shoe
8. spoon
9. banana
10. slice of pizza
11. glove
12. carrot
13. heart
14. ruler
15. envelope
16. mop
17. fried egg
18. fish
19. party hat
20. crown
21. chicken drumstick
22. sock
23. needle
24. seashell
25. flag
26. golf club
27. ice-cream cone
28. ring
29. scissors
30. flashlight

ANSWERS

1. ring
2. star
3. plate
4. stamp
5. bow tie
6. cherry
7. cookie
8. needle
9. tomato
10. balloon
11. cupcake
12. boomerang
13. horseshoe
14. hockey stick

How do birds fly in the rain?
They use their wing-shield wipers.

1. baseball bat
2. magnet
3. tack
4. comb
5. tube of toothpaste
6. banana
7. canoe
8. key
9. kite
10. seashell
11. mushroom
12. boomerang
13. carrot
14. paper clip
15. palm tree
16. toothbrush
17. drinking straw
18. handbag
19. needle
20. spoon
21. flashlight
22. whale
23. pencil
24. muffin
25. slice of pizza
26. envelope
27. crescent moon
28. ring
29. megaphone
30. sock

ANSWERS

1. ax
2. mop
3. bell
4. fish
5. apple
6. whale
7. muffin
8. potato
9. snowman
10. scissors
11. paintbrush
12. paper airplane

What did the police dog say to the speeder?

"Stop in the name of the paw!"

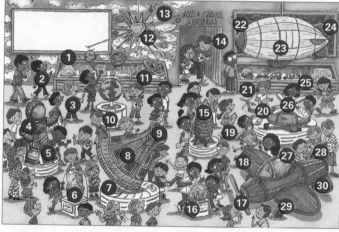

1. candle
2. ice pop
3. sock
4. teacup
5. crown
6. apple
7. crescent moon
8. arrow
9. football
10. bottle
11. toothbrush
12. golf tee
13. fried egg
14. drinking straw
15. ice-cream cone
16. book
17. baseball bat
18. cane
19. flashlight
20. fork
21. pencil
22. fan
23. flag
24. kite
25. artist's brush
26. scissors
27. carrot
28. slice of pizza
29. belt
30. snail

ANSWERS

PAGES 98–99

PAGES 100–101

PAGES 102–103

PAGES 104–105

PAGES 106–107

PAGES 108–109

1. bat
2. car
3. comb
4. fork
5. crown
6. heart
7. ruler
8. candle
9. funnel
10. needle
11. teacup
12. thimble
13. hockey stick
14. crescent moon

PAGES 110–111

1. golf club	11. wedge of orange	21. yo-yo
2. paddle	12. adhesive bandage	22. doughnut
3. light bulb	13. paintbrush	23. lasso
4. seashell	14. pencil	24. crescent moon
5. button	15. banana	25. slice of pizza
6. sock	16. pickle	26. cupcake
7. candy cane	17. handbag	27. needle
8. bird	18. envelope	28. hockey stick
9. ring	19. ruler	29. key
10. bell	20. mop	30. toothbrush

AGE 112

PAGE 113

PAGES 120–121

AGES 114–115

PAGES 122–123

GES 116–117

PAGES 124–125

1. fish
2. flag
3. fork
4. pear
5. crown
6. banana
7. candle
8. carrot
9. hammer
10. pencil
11. fried egg
12. umbrella
13. hockey stick

How do you get a cat to do tricks?
Put a dog in a cat costume.

GES 118–119

PAGES 126–127

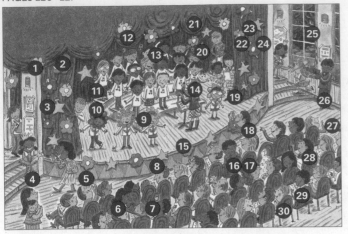

1. cane	11. spool of thread	21. snail
2. seashell	12. banana	22. belt
3. pencil	13. glove	23. funnel
4. ruler	14. fork	24. celery
5. ladle	15. bell	25. kite
6. feather	16. lock	26. tennis racket
7. sock	17. carrot	27. nail
8. ice-cream cone	18. slice of pizza	28. button
9. snowman	19. boot	29. spoon
10. magnifying glass	20. paper clip	30. saltshaker

PAGES 128–129

PAGES 130–131

PAGES 132–133

PAGE 134

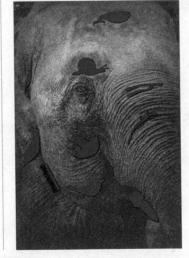

ANSWERS

Published by Highlights Press
815 Church Street
Honesdale, Pennsylvania 18431
ISBN: 978-1-64472-334-0
Manufactured in Mattoon, IL, USA
Mfg. 11/2021

First edition
Visit our website at Highlights.com.
10 9 8 7 6 5 4